PRISONER OF WAR

PRISONER OF WAR

Six Years in Hanoi

John M. McGrath,
Lieutenant Commander,
U.S. Navy

Naval Institute Press

Library of Congress
Catalog Card No. 75–11400
ISBN 0–87021–527–2

Printed in the United States of America on acid-free paper ∞

15   14   13   12   11   10   9

DEDICATION

To my friends and comrades who served the
country they loved — and did not return.

FOREWORD

For Americans who became POWs in North Vietnam, capture meant not that they had been neutralized on the war's sidelines, but that for them a different kind of war had begun — the war of propaganda. The enemy admitted to us that propaganda was their main weapon against the United States. The POWs were to have top billing in that theatrical production; a system of carrot-and-stick extortion was instituted to convince the downed airmen that "submission and repentance by practical acts" was the only sensible way to go. The alternative meant misery and pain; stating nor more than name, rank and serial number was all but impossible. The POW found himself engaged in a protracted fight, rolling with the punches and climbing back into the ring round after round. Winning consisted of establishing a credibility of defiance that precluded the enemy's leading the captive around like a placid bull with a ring in his nose.

These first-person sketches and descriptive captions written by Lieutenant Commander "Mike" McGrath, U.S. Navy, capture in vivid detail the other way of life that the overwhelming majority of American airmen chose in preference to being pawns on that propaganda front.

The reflective reader may ask: "Why go through it? Why not give them what they want? What's to prevent a uniformed American prisoner who agrees with the doves from exercising free speech? Why shouldn't the hawks bluff it and lead a decent life?"

Pure patriotism and loyalty to our Commander in Chief was sufficient answer for most prisoners. But those questions can also be answered in terms of law, common sense, and self-respect. When the Bill of Rights was passed, our Founding Fathers took note of the fact that it contradicted Secretary of War Knox's military code then in effect and decided to let the latter stand; after all, even Blackstone's

Commentaries had prescribed certain limits to the civil rights of soldiers. Our current military codes support this traditional Anglo-Saxon legal viewpoint. From the viewpoints of common sense and self-respect, what could be more inconsistent in an international conflict than committing oneself alternately to the main battery of one side (U.S. air power) and then to the main battery of the enemy (propaganda)? To do so would be at the very least to admit naivete (i.e., being duped by tinhorn "political indoctrination"), or opportunism (changes of heart behind bars are simply not credible). Neither alternative is palatable to a self-respecting fighting man.

The American pilots in Hanoi were sophisticated enough to know that all professions commit men to roles and that their military profession committed them to resistance in prison. They were practical enough to realize that good order and discipline could not be maintained without resistance. In summary, they were smart, tough guys, who, like Mike McGrath, understood the full implication of the commitment they made when they took the oath of office.

Mike is a courageous tiger, but he is a great deal more. I know him to be an exemplary professional officer and a gentleman of education and refinement who, in the darkest hours, drew on the totality of our national heritage to survive and return with honor. I think time will tell that he, and many young men like him in the prisons of Hanoi, added something to that heritage.

J.B. Stockdale
Rear Admiral, U.S. Navy

PREFACE

The Vietnam War — how unpopular it was! Unpopular with the politicians because they could neither explain it nor rally unified national support behind it; unpopular with the armed forces because they were fighting with one arm tied behind their backs, unable to bring the war to a quick and decisive end with the fewest number of casualties; and unpopular with the American citizen because he could not understand it. As the war stretched on and on with no end in sight, our ultimate goals became more and more undefinable. Divided opinions, riots, demonstrations, and a flood of anti-war propaganda further confused the country.

On only a few issues were the American people united. One of these was the emotion-charged issue of the POWs and MIAs (Prisoners of War and Missing in Action). After the peace treaties were signed and the POWs began arriving on American soil, the entire nation was stirred as the POWs spoke heartfelt words of praise, thanks and patriotism instead of words of cynicism and condemnation that so many citizens had become accustomed to hearing directed against their country.

The Vietnam War was over, at least for the time being. A few Americans listened to the stories of torture and maltreatment told by the former POWs; however, the stories were unpleasant, and most people wanted to forget.

As a former POW, I believe that ours is a story that should not be forgotten so easily. I feel that it is now up to us to set down our own record of what really went on inside the walls of the Hanoi prisons. Several other former Vietnam POWs agree and intend to publish their own experiences for the sake of history. The hundreds of incidents of torture recorded by the returned POWs should forever disprove the claim by a Communist government that their treatment of prisoners was not only in accordance with the provisions of the Geneva Conventions, but was "lenient and humane."

I felt that I could make my own greatest contribution by drawing what I saw and memorized, right down to the pattern of the bolts on the door braces (p. 9). The way we lived in the hell-holes of the Vietnamese prisons is so unimaginable to the average American that words alone are not sufficient to convey the experience. When we returned to the United States, we used the words *shackles, stocks, manacles,* and *irons*; yet many Americans could not, or would not, picture what the words meant. I hope that this book will succeed in *showing* what these and other words meant.

Hoa Lo, the Vietnamese name of the main prison in downtown Hanoi, reportedly means "hell hole." Whether or not the translation is accurate is unimportant; what is important is that Hoa Lo was a very *real* "hell hole" — in every sense. In trying to review my life as a POW, I notice that my drawings are too *soft*; I was unable to portray the actual *hardness* of the conditions we lived under — the dimly lit rooms and claustrophobia-inducing cells; the lack of adequate food which, combined with filth, caused disease and indescribable discomfort. It is difficult to sketch a vitamin and protein deficiency that results in beri-beri; and no picture can convey the impact of constant plagues of lice, heat rash, biting bed bugs, mosquitoes, cockroaches, and rats. Add to this the hostility and brutality of the guards, who had been taught from childhood to hate Americans, and the sum total is an unbelievable existence for hundreds of American fighting men who somehow survived the ordeal.

Unfortunately, the scenes I have drawn only begin to depict the hundreds of thousands of days of cumulative misery endured by American POWs. Many men were tortured more than I and suffered more than I; some died in prison. I only regret that I have not been able to illustrate all their stories.

John Michael McGrath
Lieutenant Commander, U.S. Navy

On June 30, 1967, I took off from the deck of the aircraft carrier *U.S.S. Constellation*, CVA-64, on my 178th mission, an armed reconnaissance mission over North Vietnam. After bombing a small pontoon bridge, I picked out a second target. "Busy Bee rolling in," I said, as my wingman circled to watch my run. Suddenly there was a muffled explosion. My controls went slack as my A4-C Skyhawk began to roll uncontrollably. I could see the earth rising to meet me. Instinctively I pulled my ejection handle. The quick decision saved my life, but almost immediately after I landed on the ground, Vietnamese farmers and local militia jumped on me. One man held a rusty knife to my throat, while the others savagely ripped and cut away my clothing. It seemed as though they had never seen a zipper; they cut the zippers away instead of using them to remove my flight clothing. One man, in his haste to rip off my boots, managed to hyper-extend my left knee six times. Every time I screamed in pain, the rusty knife would be jabbed harder into my throat.

After I was stripped of my clothing, I was carried through a village on a woven bamboo stretcher. The villagers were whipped up by men using battery-powered megaphones. The people were beating me with bamboo switches, pinching my skin, and twisting my injured leg. My knee would dislocate and the people seemed to get a kick out of seeing me scream in agony.

Within ten hours of my capture, I was en route to Hanoi. At a pontoon bridge, I was taken out of a truck and jammed into a narrow ditch. The soldiers who were guarding the bridge took turns to see who could hit my face the hardest. After the contest, they tried to force dog dung through my teeth, bounced rocks off my chest, jabbed me with their gun barrels, and bounced the back of my head off the rocks that lay in the bottom of the ditch.

I said my final prayers that night, because I was sure I would not reach Hanoi alive.

Immediately after my arrival in Hanoi, I was taken to the New Guy Village, a section of the Hanoi Hilton, where new arrivals were tortured and interrogated. I was denied medical treatment because I would not give any information other than my name, rank, serial number and date of birth — the only information required by international law.

I was delirious with pain. I was suffering from a badly dislocated and fractured left arm, two fractured vertebrae and a fractured left knee. The Vietnamese dislocated both my right shoulder and right elbow in the manner shown in the drawing.

I wished I could die! When the Vietnamese threatened to shoot me, I begged them to do it. Their answer was, "No, you are a criminal. You haven't suffered enough."

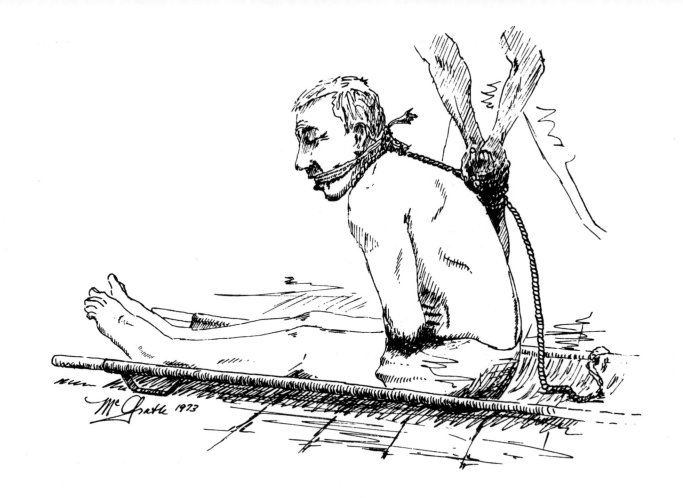

This was my room at the end of the entrance hall-way to the Thunderbird, a cell block in Little Vegas. Little Vegas, a section of Hoa Lo (better known as the Hanoi Hilton), was the result of a tremendous effort on the part of the Vietnamese to keep the Americans isolated from each other. Large 60' x 24' rooms were subdivided into eight 7' x 9' rooms in a maze-like arrangement and prevented easy communication.

After about a month, I was able to sit up to uri-nate into a rusted-out bucket. I had a high fever and dysentery. Boils and infections covered my body. These weeks of pain and misery now bring back some of my worst memories.

THUNDERBIRD - ROOM 4

I suffered in extreme pain for months. The only relief I could get was by holding my left wrist in an attempt to immobilize my broken left arm. I was delirious with pain and did not sleep for the first fifteen days because I could not relax my grip on my left wrist. I finally managed to get a strip of cloth which I used to tie my left wrist to a nail in the wall. This allowed me to relax my grip for the first time. I then passed out from complete exhaustion.

Few people can comprehend what it is like to be in solitary confinement for months or years at a time. Each minute of the day painfully drags by as you try to make your mind think of something new.

A few men were in solitary for as many as four years! One of our senior officers, Navy Captain Howard Rutledge, was in solitary confinement for 58 months. Most men were confined for a number of months, usually immediately following capture.

About twenty days after my capture, I was held down by a guard while he gave me a dry shave. The combination of my matted, dirty beard and a very dull razor blade was very painful. I later discovered that this practice of the first shave was very common.

For the next five years and nine months, I shaved twice a week using cold water and lye soap. The razor blades were always dull, even when new. Few men looked forward to shaving on a cold winter day, because it was an absolutely miserable experience.

This was one of the washrooms in Little Vegas. Men were put in alternate washrooms so they could not communicate. You were given only a minimum amount of time to wash, and usually there was not enough water. The garbage was kept in the washrooms and the pigs and chickens had free run of the garbage. If a man was too sick or weak from broken bones, as I was, he simply did not get to wash his body or his clothes until he was strong enough to make it to the washroom under his own power. Some men were placed in irons and left to live in these open washrooms as a form of punishment. They had neither mosquito nets nor protection from the elements.

My right elbow was crooked and painful as a result of previous torture sessions. As soon as I was able to stand up (one month after the torture), I straightened my elbow by hanging from a window ledge. I have not been troubled by the elbow since that time.

I begged the Vietnamese to set my broken arm and relocate my dislocated shoulder. My requests were ignored. I then begged them to let another American come into my room to help me relocate my shoulder. I received answers such as "You have bad attitude. You are black criminal and you deserve to suffer."

I thought the pain would drive me insane. I made a desperate attempt to relocate my shoulder myself by placing my cup under my armpit, and then throwing myself against the wall. I failed.

McGrath 1973

I was still in solitary confinement when the guard I called "Consumption" kicked my broken arm because I would not bow. The kick to the arm and the blow to the stomach I received convinced me that the guards were serious about bowing. From that point on, it was a point of constant resistance to try to get away without bowing if I could, and to give only the minimum number of bows whenever the guards became angry enough to take action.

For several years, room raids, or room inspections, were frequent and thorough. *Everything* that was not issued or authorized was taken away. We were not allowed to have any books (other than communist propaganda), paper, pencils, or anything reminiscent of our civilization and culture. It used to irritate me that I could not keep even a piece of a match stick for cleaning my fingernails.

During the last three years, 1970-1973, most of the regulations were relaxed. Room raids became less and less frequent and we built up our store of notes written on rough toilet paper. However, once every six to nine months we would be wiped out with thorough room inspections. Then we would start again, from scratch, the tedious process of recording on toilet paper all the information we could remember on every subject from Shakespeare to mathematics.

After two months I was strong enough to lift my slop bucket and limp to the toilet dump area. My arm was in constant pain and I had to move very slowly. I was living in the Thunderbird when I passed a guard without bowing. The guard hit me in the solar plexus and almost floored me. It was all I could do to stagger back to my room.

Bowing was the most common form of degradation that we were forced to undergo. We were forced to bow to every Vietnamese we saw, met, or spoke to. We also had to say, "Bao cao," which means, "to report," before we could speak to a Vietnamese on any subject. Anyone who resisted bowing, or who did not bow deeply enough, was beaten, or "punished."

Whenever a guard came to my room and opened the peep-hole for a security check, I had to stand and bow deeply. Sometimes the guards would open the peep-hole hundreds of times a day as a form of harassment.

"BAO CAO"

Covert messages were written on scraps of toilet paper. My favorite ink was made from crushed cigarette ashes with a few grains of sugar added as an adhesive agent. I used split slivers of bamboo as a pen, and the cap of my toothpaste tube served as an inkwell.

Notes were placed in note drops where a man from another room could pick them up and smuggle them back to his room. A good place for a note drop might be a sewer drain. A guard was not likely to search in such a filthy area.

Countless hours were spent in this position as we "cleared the hallway" for guards. Each man gladly took his share of clearing, because the conseqquences of getting caught while communicating could result in torture and months of a miserable existence in irons or "cuffs."

All the POWs became "peekers" as we followed the daily activities around camp. Everything from the movement and interrogation of prisoners to the obscene acts committed by the guards with animals, was noted. The news was quickly passed from room to room in the tap code.

Communications were the lifelines of our covert camp organization. It was essential for everyone to know what was happening in camp, whether the news was about a new torture or just a friendly word of encouragement to a disheartened fellow POW.

The primary means of communication was by use of the "tap" code. The code was a simple arrangement of the alphabet into a 5 x 5 block. It was derived through one man's code knowledge gained from an Air Force survival school.

The Vietnamese were able to extract, by torture, every detail of the code. They separated us and built multiple screens of bamboo and tarpaper between each room, but they never succeeded in completely stopping us from communicating.

"Talking through the wall" was a much more efficient means of communication than tapping. A blanket was first wrapped around a cup, then the base of the cup was placed against the wall. The blanket muffled your voice and prevented guards outside the room from hearing you. By shouting into the cup you could project your voice through three feet of solid concrete. The receiver would listen on the other side and acknowledge each sentence with tap code.

Messages were often sent from building to building by means of mute code. One man would usually have to stand on the shoulders of his roommate in order to see through a vent or over a fence.

COMMUNICATING WITH
MUTE CODE

Although our mute code was not the official deaf mute code, it worked extremely well when you had visual contact with another POW. Being able to communicate silently over long distances lessened the chances of being caught. With a little practice, one could become quite proficient.

THE ALPHABET - ONE HAND P.O.W. MUTE CODE

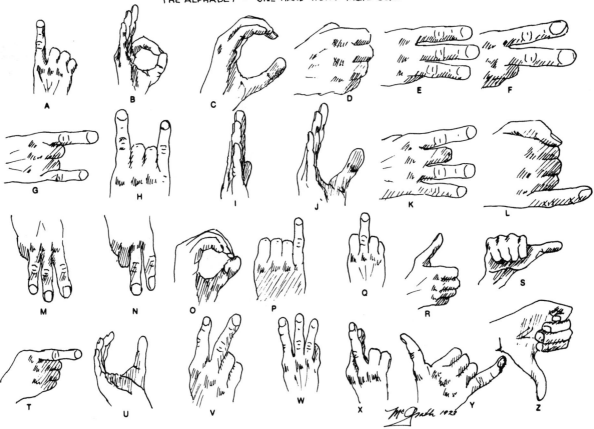

Interrogations and political indoctrinations were commonplace. The POW would usually sit on a low stool before an English-speaking interrogator. The interrogator might say something like this:

"You are blackest air pirate. You commit crimes of aggression against the peace-loving people of Vietnam. You have been duped by the capitalistic warmongers of Wall Street. You have obstinate and bad attitude. Now, the camp commander allow you to write war crime confession and condemn the imperialistic warmonger United States. If you do not cooperate, you will be serious punished."

Of course, we would refuse and take our chances. At times, the consequences were grim.

QUIZ

Interrogations were often conducted while a POW was on his knees. After several hours, his knees became flattened, red and swollen. Here, I have depicted a POW being forced to write an "apology" to the camp commander for his "bad attitude." If quicker results were desired, a small rock would be placed under each knee.

I once spent 30 hours in two days on my knees as punishment because a guard had caught me peeking out of my room through a floor-level vent.

During the summer of 1969 many men in camp were being beaten with rubber hoses and straps. One man very nearly died when he received 100 strokes a day for 9 days. Another man was tortured to complete insanity during this period. He reportedly died. The man in the cell next to me was tortured to death after an unsuccessful escape attempt. I was beaten because I asked an officer for medical attention for a roommate's infected ears. The excuse used by the "V" or Vietnamese, was that I had shown disrespect by bowing crookedly.

The turnkey would open our door at seven o'clock every morning. He would then quickly step back as the penetrating stench from nine sweating bodies rushed out the door. With all the windows and air vents bricked up or blocked off, the smell became almost unbearable. The first man out would pick up the reeking slop buckets, almost always filled to the brim. The rest of us would stagger out, thankful for a breath of fresh air. We had half an hour to wash our bodies, clothes and dishes before being locked back in our room.

Whenever we were outside the room, the guard would be constantly barking the gruff commands, "Quick" and "Keep silent!" If we were slow to respond, we would be locked back into the room without having finished necessary chores.

This is my room in the Annex. The Annex was located next to Camp America, commonly known as the Zoo. At various times the air vents were either bricked up or covered with mats. With little or no ventilation, the hot summers were miserable. The humid winters, with temperatures sometimes in the 30's, were also miserable. My socks were taken away so I had nothing to put on my feet the first winter. My hands and toes were numb for almost four months. The cold caused my right knee to become arthritic.

The standard issue items shown here included: one pair of rubber-tire shoes, toothbrush (which usually broke shortly after being issued), toothpaste, cup, water jug, fan, mosquito net, face towel, two thin cotton blankets, woven rush mat, and two changes of clothing. An additional sweat shirt was issued for winter use. The rats came with the room.

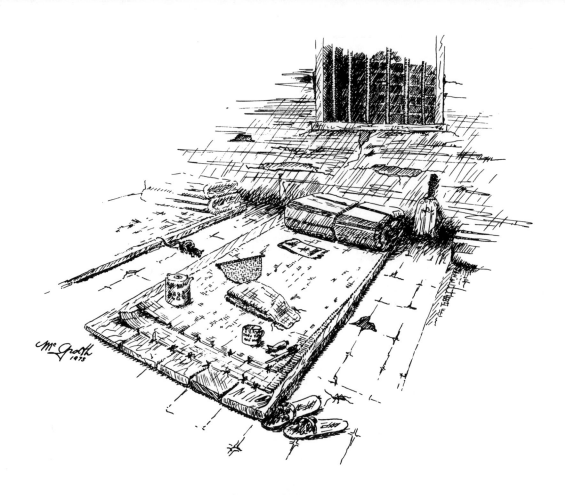

This shows one of the small courtyards of the Annex. I lived in this camp from October 1967 to August 1970. The well water seeped in from a sewage-settling pond (Lake Fester) located just outside the walls. The walls were almost ten feet high and were planned to keep each room isolated from the others.

COURTYARD – ROOM 5
of
THE "ANNEX"

Although the "V" allowed us to have three cigarettes per day, many men chose to stop smoking while they were prisoners. Others started smoking out of pure boredom and said that it was something to do. Still others would not smoke because the guards required a humiliating bow after each cigarette light was given through the small opening (the "flap") in the door.

Cigarette ashtrays were made out of bread dough. Sometimes we made cigarette mouth-pieces out of toilet paper. Each week the ashtrays and mouth-pieces would be taken away by the inspection party, but making new ones gave us something to do for the next week.

The squalor in which we lived made necessary an extreme effort to keep everything as clean as possible. We washed out our sweat-soaked clothing whenever we could. In 1967, we usually washed two or three times a week. Wash periods gradually increased to six times a week in later years. We were given a bar of lye soap and a small face towel. The bar of soap had to last from 30 to 45 days. We used cold polluted well water to wash everything. The combination of cold water and lye soap would not clean the greasy dishes, especially on a shivering winter day.

The drawing of my arm is not a mistake. It is still dislocated and appears this way even today.

Mike McGrath
1973

We standardized our names for the guards and officers to facilitate identification and communication. Names were usually picked according to some easily identifiable characteristic such as the spooky eyes and mannerisms of "Spook"; the large protruding ears of "Rabbit" (a master at torture); and the large white birthmark on the chin of "Spot." Other common names about the camps were: "Icabod," (also known as "Goose"), "Fox," "Bushy," "Elf," "Jawbone," "Pox," etc. Some of the Vietnamese came to know and begrudgingly respond to their "American" names.

"SPOOK"

"RABBIT"

"SPOT"

McGeath
1973

The atrocities committed by the North Vietnamese are too numerous to depict in this short book. There are reports of men who were burned with cigarettes. At least one man had bamboo slivers pushed into his fingers. Some men reported that they underwent electrical shock torture. The Vietnamese used two bare wires which were plugged into a wall outlet. One of my friends told of being forced to walk on his knees through broken glass.

Many men were forced by torture to appear before "peace delegations" from the United States. A POW would be tortured until the Vietnamese were sure he would read a prepared statement. The statement might read, "I have received lenient and humane treatment from the peace-loving Vietnamese."

In this drawing, a POW tries to show a member of the delegation the ugly rope burns and scars on his wrists. She ignores him because she is interested in only one thing — anti-United States propaganda.

Here is a picture of a man who has been tortured through the use of ropes or nylon parachute straps. Sometimes the guards would wrap rags around a prisoner's limbs before binding them with rope. This would prevent the marks of torture from appearing. If the "V" were careless or over-aggressive, the ropes slipped off the rags and caused rope burns. The burns became infected and left ugly white scars.

When the "V" left a man tightly bound for an hour or more, there was a good possibility that the man would suffer nerve damage in his arms and would not be able to lift his hands for weeks, sometimes months.

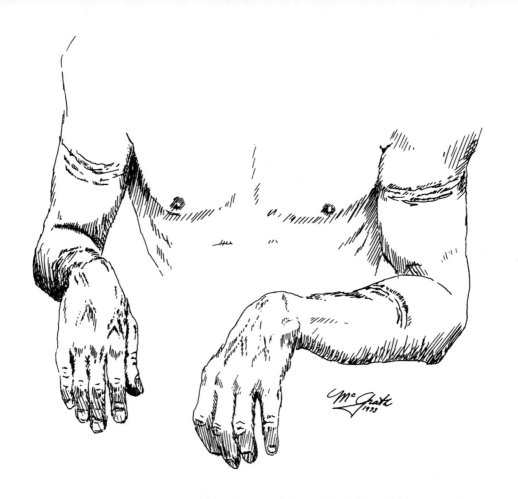

Each camp had its own special forms of punishment, which depended either upon the imagination of the officers and camp commander or upon the camp's construction. Here, I have pictured a man who has been sentenced to live for three months in the dark, damp bomb shelter dug underneath his bed. He is not allowed to use a mosquito net. The mosquitoes that live in these damp, dark holes will almost drive him insane. His hands will normally be handcuffed behind him, making it impossible for him to fight off the mosquitoes.

These are the manacles, dreaded by everyone. They were made of two flat bands of steel, with the "W" shapes hinged at one end and locked at the other. The wrist openings were small, so the flat bands would cut into your wrists, if you relaxed enough to let your elbows separate.

If your wrists were in front of you, you were always in position for a quick prayer. If the manacles were applied with your wrists behind your back, you were in for a lot of pain and discomfort. The manacles were used when transporting men between camps, but were more often used as a form of punishment. They were sometimes left on for weeks at a time.

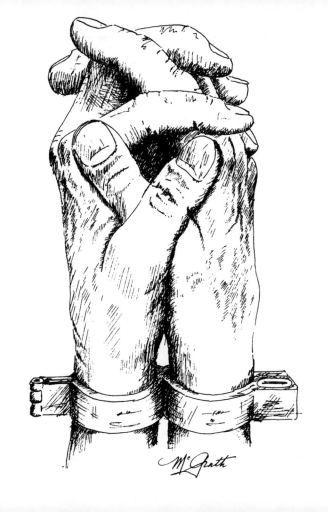

An interrogation. The guard is forcing an iron bar
into the prisoner's mouth to quiet his screams.

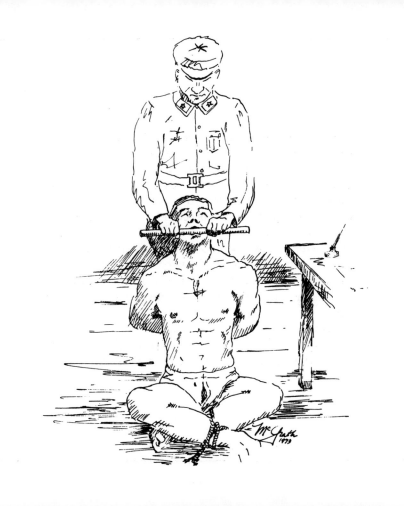

Some men were tied to their beds, sometimes for weeks at a time. Here, I have drawn a picture showing the handcuffs being worn in front, but the usual position was with the wrists handcuffed behind the back. A man would live this way day and night, without sleep or rest. He could not lie down because his weight would cinch the already tightened cuffs even tighter, nor could he turn sideways.

The cuffs were taken off twice a day for meals. If the cuffs had been too tight, the fingers would be swollen and of little use in picking up a spoon or a cup.

Hopefully, a man could perform his bodily functions while the cuffs were momentarily removed at mealtimes. If not, he lived in his own mess.

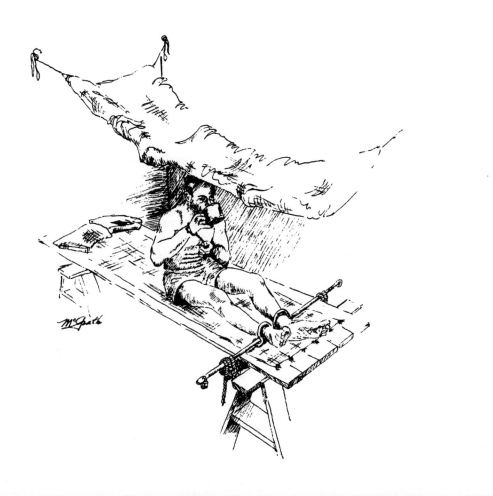

Many men were handcuffed or tied to a stool as a means of slow torture. The POW sat in one position, day and night. Each time he would fall over, the guards would sit him upright. He was not allowed to sleep or rest.

Exhaustion and pain take their toll. When the POW agreed to cooperate with his captors and acquiesced to their demands, he would be removed. Here, I have pictured a guard named "Mouse," who liked to throw buckets of cold water on a man on cold winter nights.

Some men, in heroic efforts to resist the "V," remained seated for 15 to 20 days. One man made a super-human effort to resist. He lasted 33 days on the stool before giving in!

Many of the Hanoi prison rooms had stocks installed across the foot of the beds. The base was made of wood. The top bar was of rusty iron, and the slightest scratch from the iron would cause an infection. The locking bar was inserted and locked by the guard from outside the cell, so it was impossible to pick the locks at night.

In some cases, when a man's ankles were too swollen to fit into the stocks, the guard would stand on the top bar to force it shut. This would rip the skin off the ankles and cause excruciating pain.

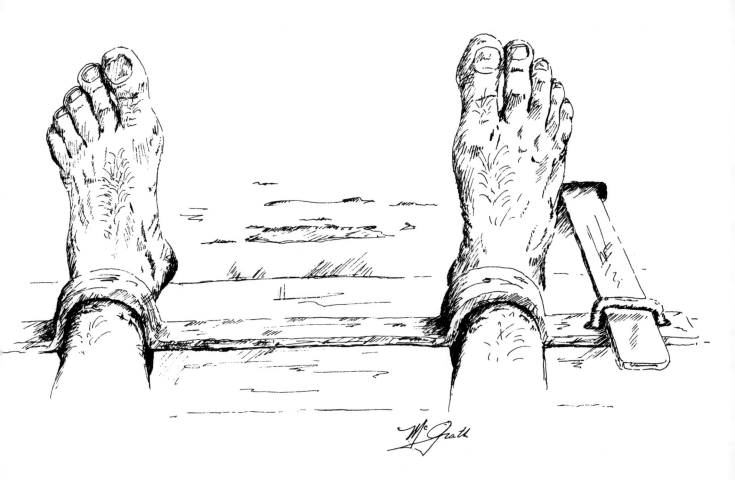

Here, I tried to depict the "Vietnamese rope trick." The arms are repeatedly cinched up until the elbows are forced together. Sometimes at this point the "hell cuffs" are applied. The "hell cuffs" are handcuffs which are put on the upper arms and pinched as tightly as possible onto the arms, cutting off the circulation. The resulting pain is extreme. If the prisoner has not broken down by this time, his arms are rotated until the shoulders dislocate. Words could never adequately describe the pain, or the thoughts that go through a man's mind at a time like this.

Many men suffered from ruptured ear drums. The guards liked to slap the ears with a cupped palm. The air pressure would break the ear drum causing bleeding, ringing in the ear and some loss of hearing.

Some men lived in irons for months at a time. The "V" would not take the irons off so you could wash your dirty underwear. We discovered that if you really wanted to change shorts, they could be removed by slipping them through the iron loops and over the toes, one leg at a time.

The unbearable pain of torture invariably brought screams from the prisoners. To prevent the screams, the Vietnamese guards would stuff dirty rags into your mouth with a rusty iron bar that would chip the teeth and tear the skin off the roof of the mouth. If you resisted by gritting your teeth, the guard would continue to shove until your teeth broke or you opened your mouth.

As pictured here, some men were hung upside down from the rafters — then beaten to unconsciousness.

During the summer of 1969, my roommate wore these irons continuously for 76 days. At the time, the Vietnamese had taken away our bed boards and we were sleeping on a tile floor. When Jim wanted to turn from his back to his stomach, he would throw the irons into the air and flip over like a pancake. The irons would bang and rattle on the floor. In the beginning, neither of us got much sleep; but Jim soon became accustomed to the irons, and I to the noise.

These iron shackles were used like horse hobbles. Various iron bars were used, some weighing as much as thirty pounds. When the Vietnamese wanted to make things rougher, they would turn the leg loops around so the iron bar rested on top of your ankles.

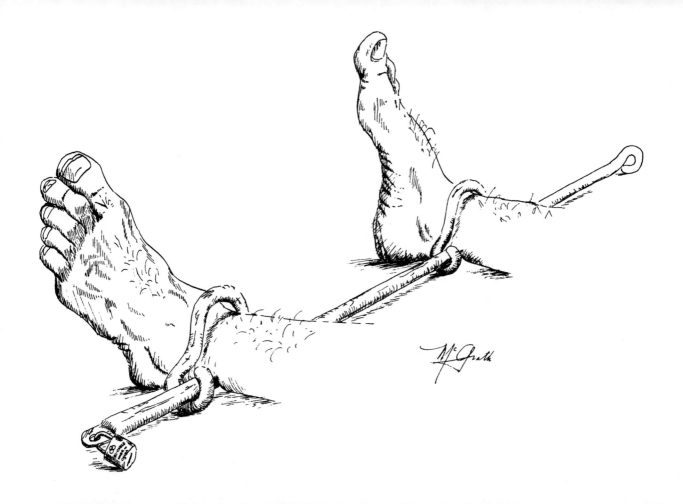

As everyone who is not limber and in good condition knows, it can be quite painful just trying to touch your toes. Forcing a man to bend, as shown here, can cause extreme pain in his back, as well as a feeling that the ligaments in the backs of his legs are being ripped right out of his body. Stress positions such as these were favorite torture methods of the North Vietnamese because of the excruciating pain that can be exacted. And just as important, no telltale scars will remain (unless the torturers made mistakes — as they often did).

After we went to bed under a mosquito net, the rats took over. They lived in the ceiling, in the walls and under the floor. The night belonged to them.

But for us, nighttime usually offered a bit of quiet and serenity in the midst of a stark, mad world. The harassment by the guards would stop, with the exception of a few security checks. If you were able to sleep on a hard board bed or a concrete slab, you might be able to get some rest before you faced the next day.

And often, just about the time you were dropping off to sleep, the jingle of keys would drive pure terror through your heart. Whose door would be opened? Who would be taken out for torture this time? What do they want now?

This is the Hanoi Honey Bucket, or Ho Chi Minh's Food Bank, as some men call it. Each room had an old rusty slop pail for toilet facilities. The top edge was usually sharp and rusty, so most men would use their rubber tire slippers for a seat. The occupants were allowed to empty their buckets once a day, usually in the morning. At this time they would try to scrub out the filth with a stick broom.

Living with the resulting stench in cramped quarters with several men, all of whom constantly had either diarrhea or dysentery, required a great deal of patience, consideration, and understanding.

We were each given a porcelain-covered tin cup. This cup and a ceramic water pot were two of the few items we were allowed to keep in the room. Each man received a little less than two quarts of hot water each day, barely enough to sustain anyone, especially during the hot summer months. In later years, the ceramic pots were taken away and replaced with large aluminum pots. This change resulted in an increase in our water ration.

Studying the habit patterns of the rats was a fascinating pastime of mine. Some rats were as big as alley cats and they seemed unconcerned with humans after the sun had set. They became very bold and brazen as they ran about the rooms looking for food or something to carry away to their nests. Sometimes they became very mischievous. They would chew up and destroy *anything* for no apparent reason. Sometimes they would chew their way through a mosquito net for a quick nibble on the calluses of one's feet or for a midnight snack on a POW's precious saved food.

When the rats were hungry, they became aggressive and could cause problems. I sometimes wondered if the "V" were sidestepping the rat problem by leaving the garbage buckets uncovered in an attempt to keep the rats fat and happy. The "V" certainly did not seem to care about the rats, nor did they try to eliminate them. One Vietnamese officer told me, "If the rats don't bother us, we don't bother them."

Our normal diet consisted of either rice or bread and a bowl of soup. The soup was usually made from a boiled seasonal vegetable such as cabbage, kohlrabi, pumpkin, turnips, or greens, which we very appropriately called, "sewer greens, swamp grass and weeds." The flavor was very bland because no spices were used. I remember one very bad food period when we had two daily bowls of boiled cabbage soup for four straight months. Occasionally we would find a small chunk of meatless bacon fat in the soup.

Bland side-dishes of cooked vegetables or fish appeared with more regularity during the last two years.

I lost fifty pounds in the first three months of my captivity. Many others lost considerably more. It was not unusual for a man who was over six feet tall to weigh as little as 120 pounds.

These are the contraband materials I usually had with me. The dice were made out of bread dough. The pen was made from a piece of bamboo, while my toothpaste tube cap contained makeshift ink, usually made from discarded blue iodine balls or cigarette ashes. A piece of rubber strap from my sandal served as an eraser. We wrote on scraps of toilet paper.

I sewed a razor blade into the fold of my mosquito net. The cross was made from a piece of bone found in my soup. I kept the cross for years. It was sewn in the crotch of my underwear. The handmade bone and copper needles were kept in the seams of our clothing. The roll of thread was sewn to the inside of my sleeve. The nail, always handy for picking handcuff locks, was kept in my mat. A piece of pencil lead rolled in a piece of toothpaste tube and a stolen box of matches rounded out my treasures.

Until 1970, exercising was prohibited. Every attempt was made by the "V" to keep us weak and demoralized. Despite the fact that we did not have adequate vitamins, protein or minerals, and the fact that we always felt tired and hungry, most men ignored the camp regulations and continued a daily exercise program. Many men give their strenuous exercise program as the reason for their good health. Sickness, such as hepatitis, could strike at any time, and it paid to be in the best physical condition possible to cope with disease.

On 20 November, 1970, a specially trained U.S. Army unit made a daring attempt to rescue some of the POWs from Son Tay, 23 miles east of Hanoi, by helicopter. Although the prison camp was found empty, the prisoners' morale was buoyed when the news reached them.

After the Son Tay rescue effort, the "V" panicked and brought most of the POWs from the outlying camps into the easily defendable prison Hoa Lo, in downtown Hanoi.

We were crowded into large 60' x 24' rooms. There were 56 men in my room. We quickly established communication links with some of our senior officers who had been isolated from us for years. Our new camp name was Camp Unity.

I made the accompanying drawing of Room 4 from a pencil sketch I made in prison, just before I was released.

"Room 4"

This is the toilet facility of Room 4 in Camp Unity. This drawing is made from a pencil sketch I made on the morning I left Hanoi for the Philippines. It shows the French-built toilets which included two pedestals to stand upon. The bucket contained used toilet paper, burned each morning when the toilet area was cleaned by an assigned detail of men.

There are some things I am unable to draw into the picture, such as the stench from the sewage-holding tank, the flies and cockroaches, and the milky-white, urine-stained floor after decades of use by thousands of men.

I was set free on 4 March 1973, and immediately flown to Clark Air Force Base in the Philippines. Hot showers, steaks, peanut-butter sandwiches and thousands of smiling faces were on hand to welcome me back.

On 7 March 1973, I returned to San Diego, California, where I was greeted by my wife, Marlene, and our two sons, John Jr. and Richard. In the drawing I tried to express all the joy and happiness my heart felt in that reunion. The years of waiting for this moment were suddenly forgotten. Then I realized how great it was just to be alive, to be wanted and loved, and most of all, to be an American.

As so many of my friends and comrades said, as they stepped from the giant Air Force C-141s to the land of the free, "God Bless America!"

NORTH VIETNAMESE CAMP REGULATIONS

On the following pages are two sets of the Camp Regulations which were secretly carried out of the Hanoi Hilton by one of the 566 American prisoners of war who returned to the United States in early 1973.

The Camp Regulations were used as a weapon of terror, being in essence a thinly veiled excuse to torture the POWs. For instance, if a POW refused to give his interrogators information on military tactics, communication techniques within the prison, or personal biographical information, the interrogators began their atrocities by stating that the POW was a "criminal" who was violating the Camp Regulations by not giving "full and clear written or oral answers to all questions raised by the camp authorities" and that therefore "any punishment, up to and including death," was "warranted and justified."

As you read these regulations, you might, in fact, see greater significance in them if you substitute the word "tortured" whenever the word "punished" appears.

The words, spelling errors and sentence structure are Vietnamese and are reproduced here exactly as they were written.

FEB. 1967

In accordance with the prevailing situation in the camp and following the recent education program of the criminals about the policy toward them and based on:

1. The policy toward the American criminals already issued.
2. The provisions of detaining the blackest criminals in the D.R.V.N.
3. The inspection and impletation of the camp regulations by the criminals in the past, and
4. In order to insure the proper execution of the regulations, the camp commander has decided to issue the following new regulations which have been modified and augmented to reflect

the new conditions, from no on the criminals must strictly follow and abide by the following provisions:

The criminals are under an obligation to give full and clear written or oral answers to all questions raised by the camp authorities. All attempts and tricks intended to evade answering further questions and acts directed to opposition by refusing to answer any questions will be considered manifestations of obstinacy and antagonism which deserves strict punishment.

The criminals must absolutely abide by and seriously obey all orders and instructions from Vietnamese officers and guards in the camp.

The criminals must demonstrate a cautious and polite attitude the officers and guards in the camp and must render greetings when met by them in a manner all ready determined by the camp authorities. When the Vietnamese Officers and Guards come to the rooms for inspection or when they are required by the camp officer to come to the room, the criminal must carefully and neatly put on their clothes, stand attention, bow a greeting and await further orders. They may sit down only when permission is granted.

The criminal must maintain silence in the detention rooms and not make any loud noises which can be heard outside. All schemes and attempts to gain information and achieve communciation with the criminals living next door by intentionally talking loudly, tapping on walls or by other means will be strictly punished.

If any criminal is allowed to ask a question he is allowed to say softly only the words "bao cao". The guard will report this to the officer in charge.

The criminals are not allowed to bring into and keep in their rooms anything that has not been so approved by the camp authorities.

The criminals must keep their rooms clean and must take care of every thing given to them by the camp authorities.

The criminals must go to bed and arise in accordance with the orders signaled by the gong.

During alerts the criminals must take shelter without delay, if no foxhole is available they must go under their beds and lay close to the wall.

When a criminal gets sick he must report it to the guard who will notify the medical personnel. The medical personnel will come to see the sick and give him medicine or send him to the hospital if necessary.

When allowed outside for any reason each criminal is expected to walk only in the areas as limited by the guards-in-charge and seriously follow his instructions.

Any obstinacy or opposition, violation of the proceeding provisions, or any scheme or attempt to get out of the detention camp without permission are all punishable. On the other hand any criminal who strictly obeys the campregulations and shows his true submission and repentance by his practical acts will be allowed to enjoy the humane treatment he deserves.

Anyone so imbued with a sense of preventing violations and who reveals the identity of those who attempt to act in violation of the forgoing provisions will be properly rewarded. However, if and criminal is aware of any violation and deliberately tries to cover it up, he will be strictly punished when this is discovered. In order to assure the proper execution of the regulations, all the criminals in any detention room must be held.

In order to assure the proper execution of the regulations, all the criminals in any detention room must be held responsible for any and all violations of the regulations committed in their room.

Signed
The Camp Commander

(Additions and or Changes)

It is forbidden to talk or make any writing on the walls in the bathrooms or communicate with criminals on other bathrooms by any other means.

He or who escapes or tries to escape from the camp and his (their) accomplice(s) will be seriously punished.

CAMP REGULATIONS 1969

American servicemen participating in the war of aggression by U.S. administration in Vietnam and caught in the act while perpetrating barbarous crimes against the Vietnamese land and people, should have been duly punished according to their criminal acts; but the Government and people of Viet-Nam, endowed with noble and humanitarian traditions, have given those captured American servicemen the opportunity to benefit a lenient and generous policy by affording them a normal life in the detention camps as practical conditions of Viet-Nam permit it and conforming to the situation in which the war is still on.

Detainees are to observe and carry out the following regulations of the camp:

I - Detainees must strictly obey orders and follow instructions given them by Vietnamese officers and armymen on duty in the camp.

II - Detainees must be polite towards every Vietnamese in the camp.

III - Inside the detention rooms, as well as outside when allowed, detainees must not make noise or create noise. Quarrel and fighting between detainees are forbidden. In time of rest, total silence is imposed.

IV - Detainees must not bring back to detention rooms any object whatsoever without the camp authorities permit it.

V - In case of sickness or sign of sickness is felt, detainees must immediately inform the camp for the medical officer to check and cure.

VI - Detainees must assure hygiene of the camp, take care of personal items provided by the camp as well as of any other thing for collective use.

VII - In case of air alarm, detainees must keep order and silence, and follow the camp regulations on security.

VIII - In need of something, detainees should address themselves to Vietnamese armymen standing nearby by announcing two words "BAO CAO" (means "report"), and should wait if no English-speaking people was available yet.

IX - In the dentention rooms, every detainees are equal with each other. Anyone does have the right to free thinking, feeling, praying etc. . . . and no one is permitted to coerce any other into following his own opinion.

X - Violation of the requaltions shall be punished.

THE CAMP AUTHORITIES

Note: This second set of regulations was issued after treatment improved late in 1969.

The **Naval Institute Press** is the book-publishing arm of the U.S. Naval Institute, a private, nonprofit society for sea service professionals and others who share an interest in naval and maritime affairs. Established in 1873 at the U.S. Naval Academy in Annapolis, Maryland, where its offices remain, today the Naval Institute has more than 100,000 members worldwide.

Members of the Naval Institute receive the influential monthly magazine *Proceedings* and discounts on fine nautical prints, ship and aircraft photos, and subscriptions to the quarterly *Naval History* magazine. They also have access to the transcripts of the Institute's Oral History Program and get discounted admission to any of the Institute-sponsored seminars offered around the country.

The Naval Institute's book-publishing program, begun in 1898 with basic guides to naval practices, has broadened its scope in recent years to include books of more general interest. Now the Naval Institute Press publishes more than sixty titles each year, ranging from how-to books on boating and navigation to battle histories, biographies, ship and aircraft guides, and novels. Institute members receive discounts on the Press's nearly 400 books in print.

Full-time students are eligible for special half-price membership rates. Life memberships are also available.

For a free catalog describing Naval Institute Press books currently available, and for further information about U.S. Naval Institute membership, please write to:

Membership & Communications Department
U.S. Naval Institute
118 Maryland Avenue
Annapolis, Maryland 21402-5035

Or call, toll-free, (800) 233-USNI.